The Wild Goose King

OpenDust™, Inc.
www.opendustpublish.com

The Wild Goose King
Copyright © 2008 by OpenDust, Inc.

Published by OpenDust, Inc.
P.O. Box 19036, Oakland, California 94619 USA
www.opendustpublish.com

English Translation: YC Liang
Editor: Jeanie Lerner
Illustrator: Tom Tsai
Layout :   Elaine Ginn
Logo: Chi-Chang Weng
Storyteller: Brian Conroy

All rights reserved.

Library of Congress Control Number: 2007936787

ISBN 978-1-60236-000-6

First Edition
1 2 3 4 5 6 7 8 9   07

Printed by Shyh Hyah International Co., Ltd., Taiwan, R.O.C.

The Wild Goose King

Translated by YC Liang

Illustrated by Tom Tsai

Storytelling by Brian Conroy
on audio CD

OpenDust™, Inc.
Oakland, California 94619
www.opendustpublish.com

Dust (Ignorance) broken.
Sutras (Wisdom) revealed.
To benefit all beings.

Acknowledgements

The story of The Wild Goose King is adapted and translated from the narrative of the Buddha's previous lives recorded in the Chinese Buddhist Canon. We appreciate the teachings from all the Awakened Sages.

Special thanks to Dharma Master Heng Lung for her kind and patient guidance in layout and publishing; to Joyce Liu and Tony Liu for their contributions in editing; to Stephanie See and Elaine Ginn for their feedback on the story; to Brian Conroy and Trisha Schaller for their valuable review and editing; to Mr. Ching-Hsing Hsu and team at Shyh Hyah International Co., Ltd. for their friendly and truly professional help in publishing and printing.

May the story be inspiring and reflect...

Kindness
Patience
Friendship
Gratefulness
Generosity
Repaying kindness
Bravery
Sincerity
Caring
Forgiveness

OpenDust™, Inc.

Once upon a time, there was a pond next to a city called Varanasi.

The pond had many fish, turtles, geese, ducks, and other creatures. Among them was a wild goose king named Jiko. He was the leader of 500 wild geese.

One day, a hunter set up a feathered rope snare.

Since the wild goose king was walking in front of the flock, as their leader, his right foot stepped into the feathered snare.

The goose king thought, "If I try to get out of the snare right now, the other geese will be frightened and won't continue to eat their grain."

So he waited until the geese finished eating. Then he showed them his trapped foot.

All the geese were frightened and flew away, except one. This one goose, named Soma, did not want to leave the goose king alone.

The goose king told Soma, "I bestow upon you the job of king, so you should fly in front of all the other geese."

Soma replied, "No. I can't."

The goose king asked, "Why not?"

Soma chanted in verse to answer the wild goose king:
"I wish to follow the king; even in death.

Dear king, you should know the hunter is coming. Please try your best to free yourself from the rope."

The goose king answered, chanting:
"I already tried all the possibilities; I am exhausted.
The rope is getting tight and I cannot get out."

Just then Soma saw the hunter as he approached, and chanted to the hunter:

"My king's feather, fat, and
flesh are the same as mine;
Please kill me with your knife,
But set free my king;
We won't harm you."

The hunter was so moved by this; he said to Soma, "I won't kill you. I'll release you and your king. You can go freely as you wish."

Immediately, the hunter untied the goose king.

The two geese said to each other,
"This hunter did something special: he spared our lives. We should repay him in a special way."

So the hunter took the two geese on his shoulders and went to the city, as they requested.

The geese were so beautiful that people in the city were pleased to see them. They gave the hunter 5 coins, 10 coins, even 20 coins, and told him, "Don't kill the geese."

Before the hunter reached the palace, he already had received quite a lot of money.

When the hunter arrived at the gate of the palace, he put the geese down.

The wild goose king told the guard at the door, "Please inform your king that a wild goose king is outside the door."

Soma followed the goose king in. They bowed respectfully to the king and then sat down on the golden couch.

The wild goose king chanted his greeting to the king:

"Is your body peaceful?
Is your country prosperous?
Are you leading your subjects
in compliance with the proper
teachings? Are you ruling your
country with an open mind?"

The king answered,
"I always feel peaceful.
I use proper methods to teach people.
My country is constantly prosperous;
I always have a fair mind without
being deviant or selfish."

The two kings chanted to each other like this for 500 verses.

At that time, Soma just sat quietly. The king asked Soma, "Why are you silent?"

Soma answered, "You're the king of human beings, and Jiko is the king of the water pond. When two kings are speaking, why would I dare to interrupt?"

The king inquired of the goose king, "I have a wonderful garden. Would you like to stay?"

The goose king replied, "Thanks, but I cannot."

The king asked, "Why not?"

The goose king said, "King, you may fall asleep and forget to protect us and we would become goose meat. When your kitchen manager can't get wild goose, he may kill us, since we would be a ready supply."

The king asked, "What do you need?"

The goose king explained, "I was captured by a hunter. However, he did an unusual thing. He spared our lives. If he had killed us, one after another, then no one would have known."

The king asked,
"How do you wish to repay him?"

Both the goose king and Soma said together,
"We want to give him gold, silver,
mother-of-pearl, carnelian, clothing, and food."

And so the king located the hunter and bestowed
upon him precious jewels, clothing and food.

The two wild geese flew from the palace back to their pond where they lived in peace and prosperity all the rest of their days.

Our other beautifully illustrated books...

    Bodhisattva and the Turtle

    The Nine-colored Deer

    Prince Dighavu

    What You Wish For

    An Old Woman's Wisdom

    Flowing Water and the Fish

OpenDust, Inc.

Dust (Ignorance) broken,
Sutras (Wisdom) revealed,
To benefit all beings.

破 塵 出 經 卷
普 饒 益 眾 生